THEIR NAMES ARE MINE
By Rajnii Eddins

THEIR NAMES ARE MINE

BY RAJNII EDDINS

COVER ART
BY WILL KASSO
https://willkasso.com/

For our children, may we choose love, truth and beauty over destruction.

Contents

Acknowledgments 9

About The Author 11

For Trayvon 15

Middle Passage 33

Blackness 36

To walk the red road 41

I want to write about trees 46

Cup Of Joe 50

Sandra Bland was right 59

Take 'em to task 65

Advice for police 72

Charleena Lyles 78

Ceasing to Cater 83

Children of Terrorism 93

Scar of Shame 101

Remember 112

Race Card 115

Happy Black History Month 116

Why we still need Black History Month 119

I Confess 124

Eulogy to white supremacy 128

These 146

I am your child 150

Ode to Fletcher Free 156

To the citizens of Bernie Sanders 160

Acknowledgments

This book has been a long time coming. It contains poetry spanning over the past 23 years. As I am now 39 that is more than half of my life. Much of it has to do with a young black man finding his voice and learning how to navigate the world in the aftermath of so much racism and misinformation.

 My hope is that it may serve as a resource to confront white supremacy as well as any dehumanizing system and to inspire educators, students and human beings in general to affirm our common humanity and to recognize the value in doing so. To take a good hard look at ways we may be complicit to perpetuating systems and ways of being that do not serve to nourish the best and brightest in ourselves. I wish to see us envision ways we may grow and change for the better and to act upon those visions.

It is titled *Their Names Are Mine* in the hopes that we may be reminded that we are all reflections and to treat each other with the respect compassion and dignity each of us so richly deserves. In light of the brutal history and present day reality of this country we all can benefit from affirmation of what connects us as human beings and use our lives to serve to create a more just and loving world to pass on to our children and future generations.

I dedicate this to my ancestors, to my grandfather and great-grandmother Leslie Randolph Eddins and Elizabeth Eddins, to my mother Randee Eddins, for your tireless love, your ever faithful belief in me, and for always teaching me *children are treasure*. By that token we all are. You always inspire me to continue to shine and this is our victory! One of many to come! I am grateful!

To my daughters Ziyah Xzandra and Amina Adesina Frances Rhoads Eddins may you always know your value and know your father loves you *Big Big Up To The Sun*. To the Eddins and Smith family, I hope this does you proud – Keep Shining!

To Carlton Langston Anderson, we got this brother, let's keep building and create our own terminology! To Will Kasso thank you for blessing the cover, looking forward to more collaboration brother!

To the Glossons, my first family in Burlington, we are family for life!
To Theaster Gates for showing how art can build and restore community,
love you for life Brah! To Major Jackson for always being a Poetry
Rockstar and continuing to bless Vermont – shine on family!
To all members, past and present, of the Afrikan American Writers
Alliance and Poetry Experience bless you in all you do for art and
community! To my godmothers Darlene Frazier and Lydia Diamond bless
you for all you've done for our family – love you much!
To my brothers in art and spirit Sherab Tenzin, Eduardo Alvarez and
Jordan Chaney let's shine lifelong!
To the Clemmons Family Farm, thank you for offering such a generous
space for community in Vermont.
To Denise Casey, Meg Reynolds, Sara Stancliffe, Jeremy Hammond your
insight, compassion and friendship I will always treasure.
To Matti Allen you are a walking gem "so figure that out" lol.
To Alpha P, King Khazm, all the epic South End, Beacon Hill and Central
District freestyles and all the wondrous artists/community builders – keep
shining Fam!
To Muslim Girls Making Change I am so thankful to have crossed paths
with you and am proud of the wonderful women you are and are becoming
– keep blessing the world with your brilliant gifts and remember don't be
Becky… BEYONCE!!!
To Young Writers Project, Geoff Gevalt, Susan Reid, Sarah Gliech and
CLIF staff/authors thank you for all the great work with youth you do, you
are appreciated!
To Barbara Shatara and Fletcher Free Library for serving youth and
community with so many vibrant resources.
To all the youth (some now grown) I have been fortunate to build and share
with, I believe in you. Remember to treasure your story and to keep shining
your light. You never know who it will touch and how far it will reach. To
you reading this, may this offer new insights, courage to speak your truth
and inspire you to find the potent power in your own story.

Warmly

Rajnii Eddins

ABOUT THE AUTHOR

Rajnii (pronounced Rahj-nee) Alexander Gibson-Eddins, simply put...is my brilliant Sun...so incisive in word mastery...his skill can slay or simply stun...while working to encourage everyone...to build and shine and get things done...

It has been my extreme pleasure and great privilege to give birth to such an amazing Word Warrior. You will find in Rajnii's latest book, THEIR NAMES ARE MINE...the thoughtful genius, compassion and astute insight of a man who leads with light...stands with courage and feels deeply for others.

I remember as a toddler, my Rajnii's first sentence was 'I did it"...proclaimed joyfully... insistently...frequently (grin) In his newest literary offering...I have to reaffirm...yes, yes...yes...you did it, my Sun...

You need to understand, Readers, I think of Rajnii as the gift I gave myself...and his gentle compelling presence...is a present to the world.

11

He is a bridge builder, a change maker...has been writing and performing music and poetry across the country for more than 25+ years.

My Sun has a huge heart, tremendous generosity, has showed himself to be unwavering in integrity and stands fearless for who and what he believes. While keeping thoughts that heal on lock...my Rajnii mindfully walks his talk...creates imagery from inner spiritual stock...and flips the script on those who'd block...

So know this--
Rajnii, without doubt... is my best work...and this book is merely another shining example of what he brings to life's table...So sit down...relax yourself...read...and prepare yourself a plate of his brilliance...Dine Well...

Randee Eddins

THEIR NAMES ARE MINE

For Trayvon, Mike Brown and the Countless Unnamed....

Lynching is not dead
It's done in broad daylight

Under the hot lights
Of media frenzy

For black blood
White guilt
White fear
And white acquittal

Where brown boys are still expendable

Michael Vick should have had Zimmerman's lawyer
Brown boys are worth less
Than black dogs

Trayvon should have been a brown lab
Maybe then we'd see more
Of a humane society's presence
If poems could March in the streets

Overturn verdicts
Bring corrupt police to justice

If they could bring a boy back his life
And a mother back her son
A father back his boy
Return bullets to a gun

Unloose the lynch rope
And unravel the knots
From choked throats
We would not be choking on tears

When do our lives become valuable
In the eyes of the law

When does hate cease
To be exonerated
Behind a badge
And lighter skin

God forbid you wear a hoodie
In the rain
While having black skin

With skittles in your pocket
You can taste the rainbow
But you can't taste freedom

You can taste your own blood
But you can't taste the rainbow

Diversity is white people's code word for niggers

You can taste the rainbow
But not if you're too dark

The rainbow may come during the storm
If you're too dark
On a block
In a hoodie
And the skittles fall from your pocket

You never taste the rainbow

Your killer has the right
To stand his ground
He may shoot you in the heart
And America may

Relive it

In sordid detail

She is only reliving her nightmare

She dreams nightmares

Often

Open caskets

Ashes

Weighted limbs

No coffins

2

His name is Trayvon Martin

Renee Davis

Kalief Browder

Corey Jones

Freddie Gray

Michael Sabbie

Delrawn Small

Terrence Sterling

Terence Crutcher

Joseph Mann

18

Dee Whigham

Tyre King

Keith Lamont Scott

Jorevis Scruggs

India Kager

Darren Seals

Alfred Olango

Ramiro James Villegas

Anthony Nunez

Deandre Joshua

Philando Castile

Alton Sterling

Korryn Gaines

Oscar Grant

Mckenzie Cochran

Jordan Baker

Reverend Senator Clementa Pinckney

The Charleston 9

Andy Lopez

Miriam Carey

Carlos Alcis

Kimani Gray

Larry Eugene Jackson

Timothy Stanbury

Sean Bell

Sandra Bland

Raynette Turner

Natasha Mckenna

Kindra Chapman

Joyce Curnell

Ralkina Jones

Henry Etheridge

Lige Strickland

Albert Sewell

Samuel Hose

Samuel DuBose

Mya Hall

Shelly Marie Frey

Darnisha Harris

Alesia Thomas

Tarika Wilson

Darius D Graves

Troy Goode

Giovonn Joseph McDade

Benzel "Red" Hampton

Ermias Joseph Asghedom

Aaron Campbell

Alonzo Ashley

Rhynell Lewis

Wendell Allen

Tanesha Anderson

Dante Parker

Tyree Woodson

Victor White

Jonathan Ferrell

Eric Garner

John Crawford

Ezell Ford

Omar Abrego

Keith Vidal

Michael Brown

Jordan Davis

Akai Gurley

Rumain Brisbon

Darrien Hunt

Kajieme Powell

Tamir Rice

Michelle Cusseaux

Jack Jacquez

Jason Harrison

Dontre D Hamilton

Ousmane Zongo

Manuel Loggins

Aiyana Jones

Kendrec McDade

Rekia Boyd

Malissa Williams

Timothy Russell

Reynaldo Cuevas

Chavis Carter

Maria Godinez

David Latham

Yvette Smith

Luis Rodriguez

Matthew Pollow

His name is Amadou Diallo

His name

He has a name

His name is *I can't breathe*

His name is Emmett Till

His name his name his name

You must remember his name

James Byrd Jr

He may whisper it in the wind

You may hear it in *your skin*

His name is guilty

In his innocence

Freedom fighter

Martyr

Trouble maker

His name

Malcolm X

Martin Luther King

He has a name

His name is black boy

Blacklisted

Blackballed

His name is Black Power

Black babies in a black market for green cash

Stolen life

Tied to a tree

Burnt at the stake

His name

Probable cause

The Negro Problem

Chalk outline

White man's fear

His name

Ear for souvenir

His name

Black

Nigger

Boy

Fred Hampton

Huey P. Newton

Medgar Evers

His name

Saves lives

Mobilizes movements

His name is watch for a Black Messiah

Bullet to the heart

Boy in jaws of wolf

White girl called rape

Whistle too free

Head too high

His name looked me in my eye

His name must die

Gangster

Thug

Menace

Stereotype

His name is

Wretch like demon

His name is take him to the iron bridge on Main St

His name

His name's legs are pulled

Until its neck

Cracks

Stabbed

Hung

Shot

Burned

Ravaged by relic hunters

His name is mistaken identity

Scottsboro boys

Tuskegee Experiments

David Walker

Living breathing Black Manhood

Heathen

Pagan

No salvation

His name is

You free nigger now get over it

Kunta Kinte

Stolen African

Strange Fruit

Stranger in a strange land

In danger of deranged hands

Enemy of the state

Genetic Dissenter

Asphalt Art

Bloody memory

Collateral damage

White man's burden

That happened so long ago

Chain gang

Wage slave

Chattel

On the rack

In the irons

On the run

WANTED

His name is arthritic hands that felt more thistles than cotton

His name is

Put your hands up

Spread 'Em

Stop or I'll shoot

His name is

BANG

41 shots

Assata Shakur

Angela Davis

Breakfast Program

Black Panther Party for Self Defense

His name is his name is

He has a name

His name is beaten severely

Urinated on

Chained by the ankles his name is dragged for 3 miles

And decapitated

81 places have the remains

His name is missing an arm

His name is Crack head

War on drugs

War on poverty

Scapegoat

Sacrificial Lamb

His name is kicked carcass

Convict

Criminal

Thief

Drug dealer

Victim

Still a child

His name will never breathe again

His name has a mother

His name is expendable

Sundown laws

Jim Crow cars

Jim Crow bars

His name is racial profiling

In court

Just call him profiling

Because *this is not about race*

His name is

Marcus Garvey

Frederick Douglas

Ida B. Wells

No rights a white man is bound to respect

His name has a title

When he *dies*

His name is *Mr. Martin*

Wearer of the black hoodie

Walker of the home path

Wrong place wrong time

Wrong skin wrong crime

His name is

Holder of the skittles

His name

His mother knows his name

Her tears spell it
In big bold letters
Down her cheeks

His name is gone too soon

His name is
Darkie
Spook
Jigaboo
Sambo

His name is different
Too difficult
To be pronounced
By thin lips
With forked tongues

His name dies without justice

Missing

Lost

Bottom of the ocean

Shark food

Triangle trade of littered bones

His name is Sun-child
Starfruit
Young Gifted and Black
But you can call him nigger

His name
He has a name
His name is the sun is rising
His name is wake uuuuuuuuuuuup

I know his name because his name is mine

Middle Passage

(Sung) There should be oceans of tears x2

This ink is not my blood
What right have I to speak

What right have I to speak

Think my words the salty oblivion
To swallow this globe

Submerging continents

Mother's one perfect tear
For her children

There were children
In that dark cramped space

Giving birth
In fetal position
To stillborn cosmos
Tiny infinites with mayhem as midwife

Below deck

Below death

Below breath was hope
Hidden in heartbeat rhythm

And now I see
Sometimes our children are
Below deck

Crammed into
Dark cramped space

But the wooden planks
Are blocks
And stoops
And streets

Still, our heart-beating hope tells me
We don't have to live that metaphor
For we are descendants of Stars and Suns
Look at the sky and see your reflection

Forgetfulness would have us think

The oceans dreamt them

But galaxies do litter the sea-floor

No one can ever take away

Our before

They sunk

So that we soar

They hung

So that we soar

They sunk and sung with tears in their lungs

So that we soar

This is not a metaphor

This is not a metaphor

This ain't no metaphor

MIDDLE PASSAGE

Blackness

Misshapen perceptions of Blackness
Dance
The speed of obsidian
Rhythm-less oblivion
Mockingly grotesque

Malformed concept of a molasses mammy
And her tar babies dancin' gaily

Noose's strings sing the melody
Black breath can't scream
When bodies swing

Dey's be just like minstrels
Dancin' a jig
Til dey feet's so burnin white blisterin' hot
That blood flood from dey souls
Like the birth nobody knows

It ain't menstrual/minstrel

But it stream strum such a purdy tune

Drip drop

So sweetly white

It shame the moon

Now the sound be white

But the blood be black

Flow flood the mud

Til the desert smack

Its lips – black hips and backs do sweat

Life stretch to gift

Death with its breath

Drip Drop

Breath Stop

Drip Drop

Breath Stop

And you are noooot

Shit

You ain't shit

Hiiiiip-Hoooooop

Hiiiiip-Hoooooop

The black blood

Blot splotch

That despite

Being a blight

Waters Snow White's desert appetite

Hatching this halo

Unholy spectrum of a Sambo rainbow

Take a swig of my nigger swagger

Clay flesh

Lacquered blacker

Than sin

Dark skin

It'll get you tipsy

Topsy

Flip the coin and opt to be Rajnii

And you'll stare down

The well of my memory

Watching the ethos

Bubble in a frenzy

Eddies

Echoes

The evil villain with the heart of

Black

Emerged from the

Darkness

Heartless

Black

Void Devoid

Soiled

Dirty

Stupid

Ugly

(record scratching)

Hip Hop

This is bloody ground

You smell the coppery cloying scent

Soil black is my royal tint
Hip Hop

I am a living urn
The ashes of my ancestors
Are my innards
Hip Hop

(lullabye)
When I am Night
And I hold the stars
I thank you for this black flesh
That surrounds my being
Nappy child self-exiled
Treasure the flesh that you're blessed in (twice)

To walk the red road

To walk the red road
To lift your heart and mind
From the fire

To reclaim your tongue and custom
In the land of your origin
Where they use your father's ashes for cement
To walk in your human skin
Where they once sold pieces

To have your survival be a secret

To place your ear to the earth
And listen

To know the elders are speaking

To be named
And misnamed
And renamed again

To walk the red road

Hear your name in the wind

To suffer genocide and still find peace within

Listen
All the child corpses worked to death for gold dust

Listen
Broken treaties and promises

Burning tipis
Pay homage
It's your birthright

Land of the free
Home of the Braves
Encamped on reservations
For our own self preservation

You know history never stopped
That whitewashed cowboy and Indian slot
You nice white-folk watched
Is less than half the plot
There's some that you forgot

Chopped body parts

Must seem like such ungodly art

When every lone ranger needs a Tonto bodyguard

It's too big

Like trying to swallow the world's waters

In one swig

It's too big

Like giving birth to the earth through your dick

It's too big

What will we tell the kids

Kill, rape and maim for gain

You'll earn fame

But don't hit

There's a reason

For this season

Of the gun lit

Were you born and raised

Where you were

Burned and razed

So much so that if you turn the page
To even speak as if concerned on stage
You may be termed reverse racist

Your herd shaken and stirred
Til you can't find a word
To name the blurred faces

Is the burning of ancients worse
Than learning to phrase it
In term papers

Does the worship
Of murderous confirmed rapists'
Lack of concern for humans served
Mirror a corporation

A severe discord accorded
Cognitively dissonant correlation

Maybe this calm patient
Complacency
With our wayward nation
Needs an alarmed rage

At least an imparted way

For art to say

Whatever's on our heart today

So walk the red road my children

Lift your eyes to the night

Those glints of light

Shine with your brilliance

When they speak of great explorers

Discoveries that killed men

Share the truth of what has passed here

And embrace your hearts resilience

I WANT TO...

I want to write about trees
But the lifeless dangling from their branches
Raise my pen from the dead

I hear their voices on the prairies
Singing in the running waters

The beauty of nature tells me everywhere
There is light

Even amidst the ugliness of humankind

And I see it in you
Even when you don't
See it in me
Seeing it in yourself

Where are Frost and Whitman
Traveling roads less traveled
Is something
We have grown accustomed to

Our roots so deep
They cling to soil
Old long before
Nature had a name

This game of cat and mouse
That fattens sows for the butcher

I sit by the rivers of my mothers
Humming songs my fathers hummed
When they were lovers

Still I want to write about trees

Not wretched countries
Dying by degrees

Oblivious decrees
To bullet ridden bodies
And spiritual disease
Hideous amnesia and hostilities
To Negroes taking knees

I'd write about the wind

But I still smell the burning skin
Upon the breeze

Even in these sheaves
I taste the blood
Upon the leaves

Tis why through the majestic
Beauty of the seasons
I mourn the morn at dawn
And grieve the eve

Greener pastures
Skies of azure I receive

I want to note the clouds of hope
That stream and beam

This knotted oak that chokes my throat
Won't let me breathe
Less I raise my pen to paint
Each limb of the deceased

I'll write my first nature poem

When with my kin I feel at home

And not a beast

Some periodic sacrifice

For them to feast

When oceans blue

Do not review

A vanquished peace

When my love is not

Returned with evil deeds

I'll plant a seed for every herb

Flower and fruit

That ever be

When that discord within the horde

Finds melody

When these brown hands dig in the soil

Toil for peace

When our allegiance to its meaning's loyalty

Cup Of Joe

These people come from low-income housing

Under privileged and uneducated

In dysfunctional surroundings

Such as these

Many times their hygiene suffers

(channel change)

These niggers is dirty

Downright vile and mean

And stupid as a block of wood

(channel change)

Would? I wish a peckerwood

Would come down my block

I'd pop 'em with a glock

For stomping where he should not have been

And cut off his oxygen

(channel change)

Now, now Miss Brown

Please calm down

Let's not become irrational

Look at me when I'm talking to you

Let's not turn *this*

Into a race issue

(channel change)

White people having grown up in white families Have experienced

all forms of racial bias

Prejudice and inequality

Qualifying them to address oppressed peoples

With the utmost sensitivity

(channel change)

Besides they ain't fit to raise their own kids

Black people are whiners

Everybody knows

Jews are the most persecuted people in history

(channel change)

All I need to do is apply cocoa butter

To the young Negro's scalp

For about 3-500yrs or so

Or until naps lay straight

And the culture abates

And the ass-whippin takes

(channel change)

Her hair is sooo fun

Wavy curly nappy

Ssssstraight

Wavy curly nappy

Ssssstraight

Wavy curly nappy

Ssssstraight

Straight up now tell me

Do you really want love to eat for breakfast

Oh, oh, oh

Maaan Paula Abdul is fine as hell

Oh you just like her cause she's light-skinneded

(channel change)

Well they skinned that nigger alive

That'll teach him to *look* at a white girl

(channel change)

The suspect is black

In his mid-life to early living

If you see this man please do not hesitate

To avoid or avert eye-contact

At all cost

Clutch your purse

And or pocketbook

And cross the street

We repeat

This man is armed

With consciousness

Warning

He may appear as a...

poet

(channel change)

If alerted to the said existence

Of racism i.e. white privilege

One may experience

Discomfort

Insidiously interwoven

With the said topic of discussion

Do not panic however

Breathe, breathe

You may very well want to cry

Or scream

Or yell out

I say do it

Yell out as loud as you can

I'm a good white person!!!

(channel change)

It doesn't exist!

(channel change)

I don't see color…

I see shapes and triangles and parallelograms

(channel change)

I watch BET

I'm not a racist

THEN

When this vile culprit tries to put you up on game

That due to the nature of racism

In and of itself

Being a system of racial subjugation

Against non-whites in every area of human relation

Entertainment, education, labor, politics

Law, religion, sex

War, war, war,

And economics

Culminating in the mass dispossession

And genocide of the indigenous natives

That founded this nation

Using this definition as a basis

If you got white skin and whatnot

Then you profit from the psycho-social construct

Struck, Struck

I struck a match in the dark

Walked up the block and the door was locked

And I ain't got no key

I ain't got no key

Can't jangle the lock open

To feel myself freely

Free myself

To feel

Every time I get close

To a lock broke

I get whitewash flooded with guilt

Then I stop janglin' the lock

Then the whispers come

BE SILENT QUIET

RARELY SEEN

NEVER HEARD

YOU DON'T WANT TO HURT NOBODY'S

FEELINGS

REFRAIN ABSTAIN

FROM SAYIN' THEM WORDS

Words like white like black

Except when followed by in harmony

Thereby remain acceptable

In appearance and character

In manner and demeanor

Everybody knows a well-mannered Blackman

As named by white people

Is a Negro

But as I said before

I can't find the space

To breathe comfortably in my soul lately

I've got too many people in my head

I've got black and white motherfuckers

In my head

To contend with

And every time I sing my pain

I feel like I'm dancing

,

Like the rushing currents and streams

Running blood and tears

Done got white folks shoes tapping

Like some snappy-schnazzy elevator music

Hip tunes to cruise to huh
Hip-hop tunes to cruise to

Music to live by

Music to die by

Music to drive by

I see them bobbing their heads
Off beat

Exchanging PC convo on the cosmos
And indigenous peoples at large
Over lattes…

"Damn Shame
What Happened To Them Colored Folk…
This Is A Damn Fine Cup of Joe

Sandra Bland was right

Sandra Bland was right
They do it in plain sight

Plainclothes death tolls
What value breath holds

Sandra Bland was right
They do it in plain sight

Bullet holes through clothes
Choke-holds and crushed skulls

You pose in your "all lives matter" pose
So cozy

But go see

You travel one stretch a road in these shoes
Whistling Dixie

When a pig sees
See if that nigger-killing trigger don't squeeze

For more peace
To police

The niggers the trigger see
The niggers the trigger see
Fricasee

BBQ niggers see
Delicacy
That's what you call picnicking

These thick as thieves
Fickle breeds
Tickle me
Pink

But look and see

Sandra Bland was right
They do it in plain sight
Really this Negus is legacy
Trick us with treachery
Lick us with lechery
Nigga please

My ministry's antiquity ubiquity
Give a fuck if you sick of me

I'm bad for your health
Like forcing a handcuffed woman
Who suffers epileptic seizures
To the concrete
To see how it felt

Yeah I'm bad for your health
Like choking a man to death
After he just asked you for help

Shooting a boy with a toy gun
Barely past 12

Sandra Bland was right
They do it in plain sight

Under the cover of darkness
Speak truth from your heart
You're in danger for life

Sandra Bland was right
They do it in plain sight

Don't let them play you
With that brother-bro-homie
Post-racial
We all could say nigger now
My family never owned slaves
Bullshit

Don't let them play you
With that *we're all human*
Like it was you who never knew it

Don't fall into the pet model minority
Swallow your pride
And die on the inside
While all around you your people are dying

And this motherfucker has the nerve to ask
Why you're *not smiling*

Sandra Bland was right
They do it in plain sight

Don't let them hinder your mind
To surrender to swine
Have you thinking just to blend will be fine
Even so-called friends want an end to your kind

So who you gonna call
When the long arm of the law
Has your throat in a death grip

911 is a joke in your town
But the punchline's on me

What a black comedy

Sandra Bland was right
They do it in plain sight

Fanning flames for a race war
As if there had ever been two sides

We need a white lives matter rebuttal
So white people don't have to feel
So much human guilt from the blood spilt
They reap benefit from

We need a true
White pride movement
There must be
Something
To be prouder of
Than accomplishments
At others' expense

TAKE EM TO TASK

These is mean old bastard lics
Drunk the last bit of Cris
And hit the last bit of swish

So grant this mean ole bastard's wish
'Cause he been makin' masterpieces
'Fore you mastered piss

This is that classic vintage
That your gramps had mentioned
Back when vinyl had style and music had potential

Seems you young whippersnappers
Ain't equipped to rip a rapper
Quicker to flip for chips
And play nigger-scripts for crackers

Shit-quick to rhyme on track
But never to track backwards
To times when niggers lost they ligaments
At picnics burnt to ashes

Hate to curb your enthusiasm for plastic
But Uzi blasting your fam quick
Uzi-blasting is tragic

While booze be passing your bladder
Who'll be passing what matters

Your people hungry for cheddar

When you be serving disaster
You be serving your maaaastuh

Undeserving of those accolades
While you whip Escalades

Teaching shorties to gun play and to drug trade
Sending a one-way ticket
To the government thug trade

Old school slave trade
New school gateway to cheap labor

And I know you need paper
But your people need guidance and need data

Crave leaders to cultivate communion with Creator

Emcees be this link
There's strength in ink
This is our chance to show what we're made of

Cause we're greater
Than luxury Maybachs and their makers
And these haters
Who treat us colder than Maytags

And they F.A.G.S.
No offense to homosexuals
That's just my acronym
For Fucking Africans Generally right on Schedule

Matter fact how you think America
Became a hegemon

We need some big payback for modern day Blacks
Origin of civilization's under attack
We been plundered and jacked
Our numbers plummet
But we keep coming back

Culture's unstoppable

Black should be synonymous with phenomenal

They tried to cut us out of the show

50 years ago

We couldn't even go to the store

Tried to disarm and coopt our flow

Like fungus among us

No one can stop our growth

Hung on trees

Burnt at the stake

Drowned in the oceans

Molested and raped

Bombed as citizens

For trying to get in where they fit us in

And lunatics poo-pooing it

Trying to rationalize

Not knowing Africans

Be the true to life

Passion of Christ

Passing the mic ceremonious like passing the pipe

Grasping the mic is like my therapy

So I don't mash in the night

Eminem got skillz

I'm not mad cause he white

More like cause they popped Pac and BIG

Cause they knew blacks would unite

Black folk under surveillance

As potential assailants

But we been here so long

We forgot how we came here

Built a nation on our backs

And we enemy of the state here

Still use our faces and skin to create fear

I swear I smoke a jay a day

Just to get why we stay here

I've known the word nigger

Since before I seen daycare

I know whites treat you different

Children got radar to hate and fear

So when you tell me "Don't Hate"

When I tell you my experience

It feels like you're telling me

To cease to exist

And when you say you "don't see color"

Don't you know it cuts a brother

To the heart

Because my skin has always been dark

In relation to white

Or light complexion

My perception is like

It's my plight

To teach whites

Like a lesson a night

I'm expressing delight

When I'm possessing the mic

I'm possessive with this melanin

I relish it

It's my better sin

Black Skin – Born Veteran

How can I express metaphor in better sense

It's like we in hurricane season

And you born in storm cellar skin

We the only Born-again

Brought from shore to shore again

As men women and children

Raised as beasts

In the bellies of ships

To the West from the East

And the wretched debris

Of this pain-ordained quest

Lives in our veins in our flesh

...Advice for police in deescalating potentially volatile situations without the use of deadly force

Pretend I'm white

Pretend white means
Human

Pretend white isn't silent and invisible

Pretend
You aren't pretending

Pretend I live in your neighborhood
Pretend I'm your mother's bridge partner
Your father's hunting buddy

The paperboy from across the street

Pretend when you see me
You don't see
An animal

Pretend you don't believe I'm dangerous

Pretend your jaw isn't clenched

That your hands

Aren't sweating

Pretend we are human beings

Pretend you care

About me

Pretend I'm white

Pretend I just shot up a church

Full of black people

Take me to Burger King

Pretend it's my way right away

Pretend I'm white

Pretend you would not put a knee

On a child's back

Pretend your silence isn't a knee on my back

Pretend you weren't trained

To see my skin as a threat

Pretend all lives matter

To you

That you don't see my life

As the color of my skin

Pretend it's not a full time job

To lie to yourself

Pretend you're not pretending

Pretend you can use a Taser

Before a gun

Pretend you can use your body

Before a Taser

Pretend you can use your words before violence

If I talk back

Pretend I'm white

If I cuss you out

Pretend I'm white

If I threaten your life pretend I'm white

If I cooperate pretend I'm white

If I'm pregnant with 3 children
Pretend I'm white

Pretend white is a euphemism

For something like
Human

Something like
Worthy of consideration

Something like
Free

If I have mental health issues
Pretend I'm white

Pretend white means
I have mental health issues

Pretend your gun is like a mirror
Now turn the gun

I mean mirror

Towards yourself

Pretend your gun is not a mirror

Pretend you are not afraid

To face the mirror

Pretend you know

We are all reflections

Pretend Tamir Rice was a grown man

Pretend you know both Jordans

Pretend Sandra Bland

Is still alive

Pretend white fragility

Doesn't cost people their lives

Pretend you are

More Human

Than skin

More Spirit

Than badge

Pretend

I am your child

Pretend you want us to live

...Charleena Lyles and her daughters will turn into wolves

...Charleena Lyles and her daughters

Will turn into wolves

The moon will howl back

And the sun

Will be your undoing

Emmett Till will come back

As Elephant Man

He will whistle

Lasciviously

At white women

In broad daylight

And no harm will come to him

Sandra Bland will stand around your bed

Staring hungrily

Her gaze will change your heart to stone

Or if already stone

Then the rest of you

Jordan Davis will return

You will meet him

In the gas station parking lot in your dreams

He will have just purchased

Cigarettes and a pack of gum

And oh yes his music will be playing very loudly

Yes it appears we are monsters

Demons with terrible resilience

And incredible strength

We are coming for your children

No handcuffs, Tasers

Or futuristic weaponry will thwart your doom

We are Rock and Roll RnB Hip-Hop gyrating colorfully

Through your black and white TV screens

It's too late

Michael Jackson already made Thriller

The wretched Negro demon rapists

Are dancing with your daughters
We have already soiled the White House
It's brown now
Like the earth our clawed hands clambered out of

We have the dark dignified audacity
To breathe the white man's air
Unapologetically

To look a white lady right in the eye
Unfazed

To not stand for the hypocritical bullshit
Of white supremacy

Yes the monsters are loose
We are claiming our lives matter
More than just on Halloween

The next time you wear a Native American costume
You will be scalped and hung
By the flag you hold so dear
The next time you wear black face
Tap-dancing in layers of burnt cork and grease

To mock our monstrous plight
It will become permanent
And none
Of your lily white loved ones
Will recognize you

You will be burned at the stake
Like only a true nigger
Or a faggot could be

You will taste
The human tears
The blood behind
These razor sharp teeth

And suddenly
The world will morph

And you will truly see
The monsters at the dinner table
In your classroom
And right beside you
As you lay down to sleep

Their red glowing eyes will surround you

For knowing

For simply knowing

That we are

And have always been

Human

CEASING TO CATER...

Sit

Speak when spoken to

Roll over

Play dead

Fetch

Let them pat your head

Make white people feel comfortable

Don't talk about racism

Nod your head

Agree

If you do not agree

Pretend to agree

Do not talk back

Don't flinch

When you hear the words

Nigger

Black on black crime

Race card

Reverse racism

Don't admit you feel pain
Or to being a human being

Lie about your feelings
What feelings

Don't mention Tamir Rice
Or Laquan McDonald
16 shots

Don't mention the litany
It's not polite conversation

Think 1950s housewife
Always smile
Keep the house clean
Hide your bruises
Don't irritate the guests
You are here to serve

Remember assertiveness
Is seen as aggressive
Smile more

Now

Wider

It makes the tears appear less

Noticeable

Bend over

Bow down

Take it like

3/5 of a man

Listen and nod and smile

And agree

I was a minority in Virginia

Nod

I have many black friends

Nod

My best friend's name was Devaunte

Nod

I loved him to death

Nod

Do not say
Black lives matter

Keep your hands
In sight
At all times

Let white people
Interrupt you
Cut you in line
Invade your space
Pretend you're not there

Now you
Pretend you're not there

Be black and silent and invisible
Until someone
White
Deems you otherwise

Cross the street
Move out of the way
Speak softly

Smile often

Don't mention lynchings
Hold back your tears
Don't scream

Just fit
Neatly and unobtrusively
Into your packaging

Stay in your place
Don't notice racism
Deny racism
There is no racism

Don't talk about Tamir
How the officers
Orbited his body
Emotionless sentinels
As he lay dying

How they tackled his sister - shackled her wrists
And put her in the back of the squad car
As her brother lay dying

White people are pure as fresh driven snow

His blood and her tears
Will only leave
Their innocence
Stained

Don't talk about white Jesus

When they try to besmirch your name
Do not return the favor

Just bring good tidings
To thy neighbors
The recipients of privilege
In a system
For former enslavers

Don't mention
Being white
Or how it is
Neatly nestled
In a nest of rattlesnakes
Do not compare

The subtle or overt support

Of racism

To trailing a nest of rattlesnakes

Do not compare the rarity of a rattlesnake-less

White person

To a polka-dotted unicorn

This year my New Year's resolution

Is to tell the truth

To white people

When they ask

How are you doing

To not pretend

I'm not being bitten

By a nest of rattlesnakes

To pierce the guise of

White guilt and white fragility

And cultivate the remedy

of human empathy

Don't tell them that

You fear your daughter

May be

Raised to hate herself

In the company

Of well-meaning

Good intentioned

Smiley-faced

Sociopaths

And their silent

Less than courageous

Counterparts

Don't tell don't tell don't tell

Racism is like the secret

You promise not to reveal

About your abuser

The one you see

Every day of your life

Don't tell them

Of your intention

To sear the word white

From its superiority-based connotation

Back to just an incidental adjective

Don't tell that it starts with thoughts

Then behavior

Conscious unconscious

Don't say what it feels like

To be lied on and lied to

Do not have the audacity

To say your life matters

In polite conversation

White people

Are like the aliens

In the movie "They Live"

If they know

You know your worth

The mask falls

I am now committing the revolutionary act
That can get a black man killed

I'm ceasing to cater to white feelings

Children of Terrorism

These are the children of terrorism
Setting sons of wrath
Set
On a War Path

Brought on
By winds of Saddam
Asking who's sane
But cursed and misbegotten

Self-defined as rotten
Spoiled rotten

These are the children that war spoils
These are the children of the spoils of
War

Contrived artificially
Assumed to consume to survive
I presume to survive to consume

No room to grow

No womb

No room for a Goddess

Holy Ghost

Don't get outside yourself

Mountains of pride

You're consumed by

Digging mommy's guts

So oedipal

You so oedipal

Motherfucking motherfuckers

Fucking nature

Till you ejaculate hatred

Talking all that be patient

You are the patients

Diagnosed with perfection

Pack your pieces hard and hot

To cover a soft erection

All the time advertising

Perfect pecs and chiseled abs

Cure-all for every ailment

They'll cure you all right
Right outta being yourself

They cure you
All the way to the bank

Hell hollywood they cured Christ
Yep. gave his meat a good seasoning

Then seasoned the meaning
Of his flesh
With their spirit less ness

Got us chasing
Man-made illusions
Glimpsing silhouettes
Of shadow's confusion
House of mirrors

Only thing is
The truth's shatter
Will get you more than seven years
Bad luck

I hope a Black Cat

Does cross my path

Shows me the math

On how white plus black

Equals subtraction

Break my people out the economic bracket

Sub-faction

Amassing

So much wealth

It's dumbfounding

While in the belly of the Beast

I hear my ancestor's drums pounding

It's confounding

This war on terrorism

War on drugs

War on bitches and hoes

Niggaz and thugz

Uncle Toms

Sambos

Mammys and Gold-diggers

New Age victims of them old lynchings

We endure for no tenure and no pension

Built this world with our hands

Of our names no mention

It's a cold invention

This whiteness as religion

Quite pissed with religion

'Cause who killed him was Christian

Now see them christen big business

While freedom getting a sentence

HooHoo all aboard

Penitentiary bound

Known for paying penalty

Brown

Why all the violence it bring

HAH! White collar crime is the thing

While they run this Barnum Bailey circus

Like Ringling

We still malingering

Depressed in this depression

Hush now class is in session

Avoiding problems sexting – email video texting

Motion for Motrin Ibuprofen Excedrin

Like seeing mama fucking
When the kids stuck they heads in
We watch the ten o'clock news
And nod off
Like it's medicine

They got off
On the death of them
Got off?
Yeah
They was acquitted
Submitted for your perusal

Tell me
Is this injustice unusual
Tell me is this profane son of Caine unusual

You will pay for your pain worshipping fool's gold
No matter how fast you run with gun
You run too slow
No matter how much you burn you cannot undo soul

Passionate for politics

But for people lukewarm

And the news serve a fix

Like it's the latest new porn

But I'd rather see midgets fuck nuns

Than see priests and nuns use church word

To fuck the children of the sun

Let's keep rebuilding till they come

Who they

The new us

The US who not intruders

Terrorizing polluters

Crossing Mother Nature

With a bloody crucifix

We got a story to rival Spielberg and George Lucas'

Original people Daddy, sent from the future

Our intent to suture

The wounds of the platoons

Of those who loot and shoot ya

Make sure you check for the accuser

And the seducer

And buy a nice pack of brew

For the Murder-palooza

Cause they just want to use ya

Fuck and abuse ya

Kill your people till you're equal

Suit boot and recruit ya

Don't let 'em find a way into your mind to soup ya

Cause they'll rotoroot ya

Decode your future

Assimilate your soul into the manifold computer

The choice is either

to be a true man or a beast

– Sankofa

SCAR OF SHAME

THIS SCAR IS A TESTIMONY

TO THE RESILIENCE OF AFRICAN MILLIONS

SCAR OF SHAME

HMPH

THAT BEARS OUR NAME

THIS RIVER OF RIPPLES TORN

OCEANS OF FLESH

TORRENTS OF RANK AND ROT

MOSAIC IN MOTION

WITHERED AND WORN ART OF OUR BODY PARTS

THIS BODY IS ANCIENT

YA DIG

DIG DEEP

I'M TALKING ARCHAEOLOGICALLY

ANTHROPOLOGICALLY

WITH NO APOLOGY TO PATRIOTS

AND I BETCHA NEVER KNEW THAT

THE TREE ON MY BACK

FROM THE BRUNT OF THE LASH

TOOK ROOT

AND NOW ITS VINES ARRAY

THE SPECTRUM OF MY KIND

IN STRANGE FRUIT

Y'ALL SEE

SEE THAT BROTHER ON THE CORNER

HES CORNERED

BY HIS OWN IDENTITY CRISIS

TRYIN' TO FIND PEACE IN CHRISTS TRINITY

HE ONLY HAS THREE STRIKES

LOW SELF-ESTEEM TELLS HIM

7 SPOTS ON THE DICE WILL SUFFICE

SO ROLL EM UP

STRANGE FRUIT HUH?!

SEEDS PLANTED

BY A GREED ENCHANTED PEOPLE
WHO COULDNT SEE PAST
MY SKIN'S VALUE
I'M BLACK GOLD
UNDER PRESSURE
MADE DIAMONDS FROM BLACK COAL

LIVING CONTRABAND

SO NOW THE CHILDREN
BORNE BY STOLEN JEWELS
OF OUR NATIVE LAND
GOT COMPLEXES

MULTI-FACETED

I'M TALKING STUCK-UP RUBY RED BONES
TO FINGER POPPIN MISTY-EYED SAPPHIRES
YOUNG BLOODS
SERVIN ROCK
TO ROLLING-STONE MEN
THEY STARE OBSIDIAN OBLIVION
STRAIGHT THRU YOU

GAZE INTO THE ONYX-FILLED
EYES OF THE YOUNG
DONT WONDER WHY THEYRE JADED

SEEN TOO MANY JEWELS
LOSE THEIR LUSTER
IT'D LEAVE YOU PETRIFIED

THOUGH IT SEEMS AS IF
WE'RE ONLY A STONE'S THROW AWAY
FROM THE PROMISED LAND

WHY BLACK FOLKS
ALWAYS WANT TO CAST THE FIRST STONE
AT THEY OWN REFLECTION
NOWADAYS EYE-CONTACT
IS A MISDEMEANOR
CAUSE EVERYBODY WANTS TO BE
JUST PEOPLE

I'M JUST A HUMAN BEING
SCAR OF SHAME, HUH?!
AFRAID TO CLAIM
YOUR ANCESTRAL NAME

NIGGERS GOT ISSUES
W/ GRADIENTS OF SKIN TISSUE
COLOR CASTE SYSTEMS
AND UPPER LOWER CLASS ISMS
CAUSE MASSA AND MISSUS
GOT MISTER MISCONSTRUED

THAT'S WHY GOOD HAIR
IS WAVY AND STRAIGHT
AND LATE-NIGHT YOU GET THAT FEELIN
JUST MAYBE YOU AIN'T
BLACK ENOUGH

TRANSMUTATED INTERNALIZED RACISM
TRANSFORMED TO SELF-INDUCED HATRED

THE MAN GOT YOU ON AUTO-PILOT
WATCHIN FROM BEHIND YOUR EYELIDS

SO THIS IS TO MY PEOPLE
BLACK PEOPLE
TO WHOM IT MAY CONCERN
YOU SHOW ME YOURS

I'LL SHOW YOU MINE
YOUR BLACKNESS THAT IS
SPIRIT SHINE
DOWN THE WHEEL OF TIME
SOULCLAP AND ALL

AM I BLACK ENOUGH 4 U

HAD MY KOOL-AID IN A PLASTIC BAG
IN THE BACK OF THE CLASS
AND 1 RED-SOAKED FINGER

AM I BLACK ENOUGH

MY AUNTIE WAS ON CRACK
AND MY UNCLE WAS AN ALCOHOLIC
AND MY MAMA WAS ON WELFARE
AND SHE MADE BLACK MAGIC

TO KEEP ALL US 5 KIDS
FROM GOING TO HELL IN A HAND BASKET

MY GREAT-GRANDMOMMA
COULD MAKE PEACH COBBLER

FROM SCRATCH
NOW HOW BOUT THAT

I GREW JAMMIN TO AL GREENE
AND AL JARREAU
AND I LEARNED ABOUT AL JOLSON

TELL ME AM I BLACK ENUF 4 U

I'M NOT TRYIN TO SAVE FACE

SHEEIT IM'MA TAKE YOU BACK
TO THAT SACRO SANCT
BLACK SOUL PLANE
JUST BENEATH
THE UNDERGROUND RAIL-ROAD
YOU GOTTA PAY THAT THERE TOLL
TO WEAR THAT BLACK GOLD

VIBING TO FREEDOM-BELL HOOKS
THROWIN' UP THE CORNEL WEST COAST!!

UNTIL HELL SHRINKS
INSIGNIFICANTLY

INTO THE BLACKGROUND

INDISTINCT TO EXTINCTION

WE SQUASH OUT THAT INSECTILE VOICE
CHALK IT UP
TO BE NOTHING BUT
UNINTELLIGIBLE WHITE NOISE

OH I'M GON' TAKE YOU BACK
TO THAT SACRO SANCT
BLACK SOUL PLANE
WHY DOES OUR SCAR OF SHAME
MEAN THIS SUPER POWER'S ACCLAIM
WE MUST RECLAIM OUR NAME
TO SEE OUR PURPOSE ORDAINED

SO WHO AM I?
THAT PIMP THAT MANDINGO
SON OF MAMMY
SAMBO TAR BABY JIGABOO
OR THAT SAME OL' NIGGA WHO GOT GOT
COOKED INSIDE THE MELTING POT
TO MAKE NIGGA-STEW

AMALGAMATION

101 BLACK SPOTS
TO COVER UP THIS WHITE DOG
LIKE A DALMATIAN

EBONY AND IVORY MADE TOPAZ
AND IF'N YOU AIN'T CLOSE TO MASSA
YOU GETS NO PASS
FOR YA BROKE ASS

SO WHO AM I
CHILD OF THE SCAR OF SHAME
LOVING MY FLESH RELIGIOUSLY
LOVING MY SOUL CONTINUOUSLY
THIS SCAR OF SHAME
IS MY PRIDE AND GLORY
FOR IT SHINES
WITH ALL THE BRILLIANT FLAME
THAT IS OUR HISTORY
SO WHAT CAME FIRST
THE COLORED OR THE NEGRO
NEITHER – *NEITHER*

EENY MEENY MINY MOE
BEFORE IT WAS CATCH A TIGER
WAS CATCH A NIGGER

AND ANY NIGGER WOULD DO
MULATTO MESTIZO
HIGH-YELLA HALF BREED TOO
LIGHT BRIGHT DAMN NEAR WHITE
BUT NOT QUITE

RICH POOR OR INDIFFERENT
ALL IT TAKES IS ONE DROP
TO FIT THE DESCRIPTION
PROFILE FOR YA MUGSHOT

NIGGERS GOT GRADIENTS
FROM MIDNIGHT BLACK
TO PAPERBAG PASSING

NIGGERS GOT GRADED
A+ IF YOU STAY PUT
AND KNOW YOUR PLACE

BUT REALLY NIGGERS GOT DEGRADED

DEMOTED
FROM HUMAN BEINGS
TO INHUMAN BEASTS
YOU COULD DO ANYTHING TO
JUST FOR SPORT
...AND ENTERTAINMENT

SO HUMOR ME
IN THIS TRAGIC COMEDY
WHERE SOME EQUATE PROXIMITY
TO WHITES
WITH SOME SEMBLANCE OF EQUALITY

**"IF YOU DO NOT UNDERSTAND WHITE
SUPREMACY (RACISM)
WHAT IT IS, AND HOW IT WORKS,
EVERYTHING ELSE THAT YOU DO
UNDERSTAND WILL ONLY CONFUSE YOU."
DR NEELY FULLER JR**

Remember

I WANT TO SPEAK TO THE WORLD'S MINORITY

GREAT AND SUPERIOR CIVIL LIARS (CIVILIZERS)

THE WEAVERS OF RACE AND ETHNICITY

INTO A PSEUDOSCIENCE

OUR WAYWARD COUSINS

WHO NOW WISH TO BE

HEADS OF HOUSEHOLD

OF THE HUMAN FAMILY

LET ME EXPOSE THE TENDER WHITEMEAT

HIDDEN FROM LIGHT SO LONG

AND SAY SOFTLY

AS NOT TO BRUISE ALABASTER FLESH

WITHIN AFRICAN HISTORY

LAY THE MISSING PAGES

OF WORLD HISTORY

RETURN TO YOUR PAST

TRACE THE RAGGED EDGES

OF UNTOLD EPICS

CLAIM THIS ANCESTRY AS OURS

THAT WE MAY KNOW

OUR TRUE IDENTITY

CUT ETHNOSPECIFIC ARGUMENTS

TO THE QUICK

IT IS ONLY FITTING

HERE IN THE SELF PROCLAIMED CITADEL OF JUSTICE

DEMOCRACY AND FREEDOM

AMERICA

HOME OF THE BRAVE AND FEARFUL

THE INNOCENT AND THE CONFLICTED

WAYWARD LIBERAL

AND THE BLATANTLY COMPLICIT

AMONG YOU BE WHERE I TAKE MY STAND

THEY KEEP TELLIN' ME

WE'RE ALL HUMAN BEINGS

LIKE ITS NEWS TO ME

MORE FOR THEIR SAKE THAN MINE

KEEP SAYIN'

I'M SO ARTICULATE

HOW I SPEAK SO WELL

DID I WRITE THAT MYSELF

HOW DO I REMEMBER

ALL THOSE WORDS

I WANT TO SCREAM TO TELL THEM

BEFORE EUROPE HAD A POT TO PISS IN

OR A WINDOW TO THROW IT OUT OF

WE WERE MILLENIA OLD

YOU HAVEN'T BEEN LITERATE TOO LONG

REMEMBER A TIME

WHEN THE DARK CONTINENT YIELDED

MANY AN ENLIGHTENED SOUL

MANY A WEARY TRAVELLER

KNELT AT THE FEET OF ELDERS

EAGER FOR JEWELS TO BEHOLD

Race Card

THE RACE CARD IS ONLY A CLICHE

TO NEGATE ANY DEBATE

OVER WHITE SUPREMACY

NO MEMBER OF THIS HUMAN RACE IS UNMIXED

NO WONDER WE ALL STRUGGLE FOR IDENTITY

Happy Black History Month

I can't keep up
Nobody sent me the memo
I can't even front

I was under the impression
This was still Black History Month

But with utter awe and dismay
The white man self-proclaimed
"African" relates

That from the dates
Feb 1st – Feb 28th

Is no longer to be
Black
In fact
History month

He asserts the imperative
Hunch in his narrative

It is now African American history month

That mystery month

Of 28 days

Where every black leader

Oh excuse me dear reader

Every African American leader and artist

& teacher & preacher guest speaker regardless

Is called from the woodwork

For 28 days

To celebrate African American praise

But I friend

However

Was quick to respond

This year 29 days we celebrate on

One day for the leap year

One extra what glee here

But see here

I choose not to limit

But celebrate the infinite

Dates black people may be here

So politely to the whitey

With arrogant scoff

Happy Black History Month And Fuck Off

Why we still need Black History Month

Don't be so fearful

Of being racist

That it deludes your common sense

Or so fearful of racism

Existing

You become a hypocrite

I wrote this on the off chance

There would be some black people

Who love themselves

Enough to listen

In the audience

Or some white people

Who know black folk

Exist

In more than convenient moments

Or just some human folk who love truth

And have enough sense

To care about they roots

The librarian asks me
Why do you think
We still need Black History Month

For the same reason that Texas
Calls slavery
Unpaid internship

Because the evil
Of ignorance and racism
Must be vigilantly opposed
With truth love and sincere inclusion
Because it was once Negro History Week

And for the children
Who daily see themselves
Thru the lens
Of stereotypes

And those who only know
Television
As relationship
To black people and people of color

For my daughters
Who are growing
And will not be
Choked out
By the diminishing
Of our value

For the legacy of our people
That makes American ideals
A sought for reality
Rather than
A cliché banality

For you
For your spirit and your conscience
So it doesn't putrefy
In the delusion of denial
And fear made religion

Because
Black People
Must not become history
Our story
Is a part of your story

The beauty

Wonder

Triumphs and trials

Need to be known

Sung from the hilltops and mountain peaks

Resounding in the valleys and grass plains

Echoing down the alleyways and boulevards

Because black red brown yellow

Are the colors of my true love's hair

And the Universe

Because beauty and truth

Will not be contained

Because these are our ancestors

We owe them a debt

Of gratitude

Because LOVE will not be silenced

Because teaching white supremacy

Is poison

We are all

Still recovering

Conditioned to tolerate it

In small doses

The human family must heal

Soon this sickness

Will be vomited

And all that will remain

Will be you

Beautiful

Healthy

Free-minded

You

Think of it

As your chance

To celebrate the human family

In preparation

For making every day our celebration

I Confess

I confess

I've killed a white man

And a white woman

A couple

As innocent

As they both may appear

You must know

They were both

In the back

Of my head

They'd been placed there

Ages ago

Whispering

Watching

Giggling

Guffawing

I could hear their glasses

Tinkling

Their petitely protected pink toes

Resting gently

As they steered my gaze to and fro

I found them in their sleep

Tipsy off some foul

Concoction of black blood and white wine

I had a Nat Turner moment

Put on my hard nigga suit

Took off the eloquent acceptable black man

Picked up the rusty machete

Left in the fields of my mind

Picked it up like

Some sword in the stone myth

And chopped and chopped and chopped

Until nothing I saw was

Recognizable

I chopped until I could hear my own voice

In my voice

I chopped until

The metal clanging rang bells

Leaving a thousand slain hells

From our distorted shells and murdered selves

It was then I was finally released from my cell
With all my inmates sipping blood of wardens
From bloody holy grails

Now we feast on the pale frail
And dance a million midnights
While our suns burn where they dwell

It's only fair

This bloody tear
As right as rain and breath and air

It's like when Langston said
Life ain't been no crystal stair

Or when Malcolm wrote
His first chapter nightmare

There are some things that have to be written
In blood
So the flesh can hear

What deaf ears could not
There are some passages
That are best recited
In blood curdling shrieks
And as passages are
Swam in

Bathed in

A red frenzy

Centuries of carnage
Reborn into pristine massacre

For every child ripped from womb
And crucified at birth

There are many songs to sing
And this is one
I am learning

Eulogy to white supremacy

White supremacy will protect itself at all costs
Will yell at you at the bar about not being satisfied
With white people's conduct
Then take you home and tell you how offended it is

How grateful you should be
For all it's done for you

White supremacy refuses to listen
Without interruption
White supremacy always makes it about itself

White supremacy thinks some prison time
Is equivalent
To generations of slavery

White supremacy listens
To reggae and hip-hop
Plasters BLACK and Brown faces on the wall
But cannot tolerate
Being called on white supremacy

White supremacy refuses to acknowledge

BLACK and Brown people's experience

Without comparing it to their own

White supremacy refuses to be accountable

Or to make a plan for transformation

White supremacy recoils in close proximity

White supremacy cannot afford

To recognize BLACK Brilliance without tokenizing

White supremacy plays the victim

White supremacy witnesses micro-aggressions

And says nothing to the aggressor

White supremacy is obsessed with scarcity

White supremacy fears the power

Of BLACK Women and Mother Nature

White supremacy plays innocent

White supremacy is silent on race til it's convenient

White supremacy is not really white
It's 3% Native American on its mother's side

White supremacy can decide to be Native
When it's convenient
While sterilizing actual indigenous people

White supremacy so to speak
Has no skin in the game
White supremacy expects
BLACK people and people of Color
To be subservient or self-effacing
Or at least non-confrontational

White supremacy sees assertiveness
In BLACK People and people of Color
As aggressive and attacking

White supremacy is weak

White supremacy experimented
On enslaved African Women
To *father* gynecology

White supremacy is a *motherfucker*

White supremacy cut off the genitals
Of BLACK Men and put them in their mouths
Or kept them
As souvenirs

White supremacy was afraid of mongrelization
White supremacy calls murdering BLACK People
In cold blood
Riots

White supremacy calls BLACK People rebelling
Against BLACK People being murdered
Riots

White supremacy is adopting
BLACK People and people of color's children
Like hot cakes

White supremacy is not capable of teaching
BLACK and Brown children
To be their best and brightest selves

White supremacy is honestly not interested in this
White supremacy is interested in replicating itself
In the minds of
BLACK and Brown children and people

White supremacy knows blue eyes
Blond hair and white skin
Are the only standards for beauty

White supremacy can consider itself progressive
While stewing for having to serve me

White supremacy thinks passive aggressive service
Is satisfactory

White supremacy thinks Stephon Clark,
Diante Yarber, Sandra Bland, and Tamir Rice
Are isolated incidents

White supremacy thinks if BLACK people
Were more polite
And just listened to police
They would be killed less
White supremacy is tired of hearing this poem

White supremacy is tired of hearing about race

White supremacy scalped BLACK people
And cut off their ears
And threw them into rivers
Chanting for them
To swim back to them damn Yankees

White supremacy will
Mortally wound a BLACK man
Jump on his chest
Plunge a knife into him
Smash his body with stones
Then cheer as children watch

White supremacy caused Lincoln to say
But for your race among us there could not be war

White supremacy will stab, club and shoot
BLACK boys
Then chain them to trees
For the crime of being
BLACK and free
White supremacy made the Black Codes

White supremacy calls people

Who were formerly enslaved

Lazy and idle

White supremacy allowed Mississippi

To delay ratifying the 13th Amendment until 2013

White supremacy will hear you say

Your family has been

Lynched

Murdered

Raped

And be offended by

You telling it what it already knows

White supremacy is sensitive

White supremacy will be more offended

By this poem than white supremacy

White supremacist gives people things

Then takes them away

But calls Native Americans Indian givers

White supremacy wants to focus the conversation

On being called racist and not eradicating racism

White supremacy spells and says your name

Incorrectly

Repeatedly

On purpose

White supremacy doesn't see any connection

To articles on slavery and white people's complicity

White supremacy says

You are preaching to the choir

White supremacy will talk over you

While claiming to be listening

White supremacy knows all about slavery

White supremacy knows about Rastafari

So it knows more about experience than you do

White supremacy will touch your hair then ask to touch your hair

White supremacy doesn't have good boundaries

White supremacy smiles awkwardly

White supremacy is curious about you

When it is convenient

White supremacy is the rule not the exception

White supremacy cloaks itself in terms such as
Liberal or progressive
As a barometer
Of how less racist it is
Than its forebears

White supremacy knows racism doesn't exist
White supremacy has amnesia
White supremacy knows this isn't about race

White supremacy doesn't see color
Has black friends
Classmates, siblings

White supremacy can say nigga without the e r

White supremacy is raising its children to be
Obtusely comfortable with racism

White supremacy doesn't like to face its reflection
When the light of truth is on

White supremacy would rather be comfortable
While people die than change

White supremacy secretly thinks
BLACK people are dysfunctional

White supremacy thinks BLACK people
Are dysfunctional
Period
With no apology
White supremacy is helpless to change itself
White supremacy is passively against
White supremacy

White supremacy thinks this is enough
To change white supremacy

White supremacy doesn't really want to change white supremacy
But only to not be called racist

White supremacy is scared of the dark
White supremacy is scared of the dark
…races
White supremacy is afraid to face its dark past

White supremacy is afraid
White supremacy is afraid of genetic annihilation

White supremacy prefers BLACK culture
To BLACK people
Unless they collude with
White supremacy

White supremacy does not like me
Telling its business

White supremacy does not like when I call it out
Speak my truth
Remain intelligent
Tell my story unflinchingly

I would call white supremacy a bitch
But that would be disrespect to female dogs

White supremacy thinks awareness of its ignorance is sufficient
White supremacy would rather support
A pathological liar to retain white supremacy
Than think for itself

White supremacy wants

BLACK people and people of color

To be satisfied with pseudo lukewarm acceptance

White supremacy is the Borg

White supremacy is right even when it's wrong

White supremacy is never wrong

White supremacy will not want to

Discuss this afterwards

White supremacy thinks white tears

Are of more concern than

Genocide, Colonization

Conquest, Capitalism and Institutional Racism

White supremacy is incorrect

White supremacy is dying

White supremacy is on its last legs

White supremacy is doomed

White supremacy is a snow flake in the desert

White supremacy is a suicide pact

White supremacy has an inferiority complex

White supremacy knows
True hueman beings will outlive it
White supremacy wants to distract you
From the joy of living
With white supremacy

White supremacy is degrading to all huemanity
White supremacy is insulting
To all intelligent beings

White supremacy is a psychotic child
That kills all its playmates to rule a sandbox
White supremacy would rather see the world burn
Than share

White supremacy is colorless and odorless
But just as deadly as carbon monoxide

White supremacy sent Lorraine Hansberry
And her father to an early grave

White supremacy is a great pretender

White supremacy thinks America is different than

Germany and South Africa

White supremacy is a liar drunk on its own lies

White supremacy is a thief

That thinks it is generous

To loan back stolen artifacts

White supremacy fears the truth

As vampires do sunlight

White supremacy is the only terrorist

That can use mental illness

As a cop out

White supremacy is a mental illness

White supremacy sees

BLACK people and people of color

When it chooses to

White supremacy

Uses the victims of white supremacy

As scapegoats for its own inadequacies

White supremacy kills without consequences

White supremacy is a murderer
That seeks to make its victims
Responsible for their own deaths

White supremacy uses people of European descent
As carriers for its viral sickness

White supremacy fears BLACK genius
Will rise in the form of a BLACK messiah

White supremacy would rather poison its own children
Than correct its behavior
White supremacy has a God complex
And is afraid of the spiritual power
Of BLACK People and people of Color

White supremacy has been trained well
To mock the death and intentional undermining
Of BLACK people and people of Color

White supremacy worships Hitler

White supremacy assassinates freedom fighters
Then makes of them martyrs and stamps

And street names

White supremacy is a manmade construct
And as such can be unmade

White supremacy we are coming for you

White supremacy we are uprooting you
From the minds
And hearts of the people
White supremacy love is stronger
Than your temporary hold on us
White supremacy you cannot hold us much longer

White supremacy you are an invention
Of vilely short-sighted men

White supremacy you are a maniac
And your rampage will soon end

White supremacy your sociopathic reign is at an end

White supremacy our children are much brighter
Than you can dare to dream

White supremacy you were sick to begin with
And I am glad you are dying

White supremacy I have no qualms
About killing you in your sleep
Because through your death
The people will awaken
White supremacy the disdain and contempt
You show for me
Is a reflection of your own self repugnance

White supremacy the grimace after the smile
Is not a good look

White supremacy you suffer
From a terminal case
Of limited imagination

White supremacy that's why poets and artists
Are your arch-nemesis

White supremacy we are coming
With love and undiminished brilliance
As sword and shield

White supremacy we will not be silent or silenced

White supremacy you were a bad seed since infancy

White supremacy your ass is showing
Your lunacy has nothing to do with the moon
Only time and lies and bad habits

White supremacy you are a froth of
Pumped up delirium and self-importance

White supremacy
Your dictionary based delusions of innocence
Will not save you

White supremacy nothing and no one can save you

These (for us and those we mourn)

This breathing beating heart

These eyes

Glowing

A window to a soul that sparks

These hands

That held and warmed and made

These tongues

That spoke

These lips

That praised

Sincere in gratitude and grace

These arms

That waved, warmly embraced

These legs

That walked

These feet

That ran

These teeth

That smiled wide and grand

These cheeks

That were for tears to roll

And also laughter

Fierce and bold

These shoulders

That could hold a head

These knees

That bent

For prayer and bread

These voices

That did give life song

And cried and cheered

And whispered calm

These chins

That lifted

To the sky

These fingertips

That made pen fly

These limbs

And bodies

Temples pure

How sad that they are now no more

How many more must die before
We marvel that each life endures

How many must we mourn and grieve
Before we truly see our strength
Lies in the truth that all are bound
All sacred holy forms abound

That every color shape and hue
Every temple holds a pew

From which a common spirit views
All midnight moons and morning dews

That every single one is strand
Connected to a greater hand
From which all life and breath expand
A universe in ancient dance

For all are family yet far flung
To see otherwise is mute and numb

It silences the oceans roar
And keeps our journeys on one shore

For there is splendor

Ever more

In every mortal

Ever born

I Am Your Child (for turtle)

I am your child

The one with the blondish curls

The green eyes

And light enough

Skin

To still be seen

As pretty

I am your child

You told me I was pink

And you kept me

Away from

My darker skinned family

I am your child

You tried to make my father

Into a stereotype

You told me he was working

A lot

And that was why I couldn't see him

You made me say he poked me

And told me it was just a story

I am your child

You lied to me

And on my father

You got a restraining order against him

Saying he was following you

And staring

At you and my stepdad

He spent a day in jail for saying hi to me

My stepdad even got a trespass order against him

For bringing me back to you both

You both knew

You could use your skin's privilege

To be believed

And you exploited that

But you never knew

My dad would never give up

I am your child

You never knew how much

My father loves me and that even

In the brief windows

You allowed us to be together

We made magic memories
And widened those windows
Into doorways
We made songs that people
All over the world saw
And shared with their children

And all that time
You were too jealous
And insecure
To see the beauty
To be happy for the Joy
We shared together

I am your child
And I am growing older everyday
One day I will know all these things
And I will confront you about them
And what will you say
When neither lies, white skin, gender, or title
Will shelter you from accountability
Will you finally apologize
To me
To my father, to my grandmother

Will you cry tears for absolution

Beg my forgiveness

And tell me

Of your mother

Who abused you

How you never confronted her

And it left you

Wounded

And still reeling

Too heavy laden

With the pain

And unresolved anger

To see clearly

That you were harming me

By depriving me

Of my father

And my family of color

What will you say then Mama

I am your child but I am his too

I love my father

We sing songs and make stories

And make music

And one day soon
The whole world will know it
The whole world will rejoice in our reunion
And will laugh and sing
A world-wide refrain

We will share new stories
And make new songs
And sit and smile a good long while

And all the obstacles you put up
Will be as
The blink of an eye
The flash of one lash
Water under a bridge
That we've now traveled past

I am your child
But I am more than your own
I am not property
Or commodity
To be bought traded and sold
To be hoarded as some item
Only you have bestowed

As it turns out

I am also my father's child

I share his silly sense of humor

And even his smile

His penchant for music

And playful freestyle

And when all's said and done

We will sit back and smile

Make more memories spun

As we laugh a long while

As we laugh a long while

Ode to Fletcher Free

Dear House of Stories
You house our stories
You hold so many tales
Of the head and heart
On and off your shelves
My story has joined with yours

Now it sings a song

You remember
When I was holding my child
In these arms
Singing her all of my hopes

Catching each tear
In a sphere
With each note

How you held us
In your warm and solemn silence

You still let our voices
Echo on entrance

Now whenever we traverse
That sacred boundary
Our voices become tinged
With reverence

And you still have room
For all the children's laughter

I love your nooks and crannies
Where the beleaguered
And winter weather-worn
Go to nest
Finding brief respite from living storms
And their own torn pages

Carnegie spoke of you
"An oasis
in the desert"
He called you
Still I wonder if he ever knew

How sunlight would stream majesty
Through the eye of your colored glass

How librarians
Would trace their own stories
And oh how the Poetry would ring

Bounding off
Autobiography and Fantasy

Reverberating through
Encyclopedias
Cookbooks and fables

You
Safe-keeper of Imagination
Childhood's Angel

Last week I blew bubbles into magic memories
Watching puppets dance
No strings attached

I found my youngest daughter

Again

And again

In book shelves

As well as just

Adjacent

To the staircase

This is why

I know

Our story is

Unfolding

To The Citizens of Bernie Sanders
& The Green Mountain State

Addition taught me
To count the money stolen
The hungry and poor
The rising death toll

Subtraction
Like one starkly cut throat
What to take away
And minus

Collateral damage
After the gun smoke

Multiply
The products made by
Imprisoned hands
By the prices they command
Silent wars over stolen land

Divided we fall united we stand
Division is a conquerors plan

And I hope you're not listening

That you leave this place
Lily white and safe and post racial
That you count your black friends
And your white friends
And your lucky fucking stars
For where you are
Land of Bernie Sanders
Cake walks and Green Mountain manners
Where nigger is said politely
With pure New England standards

Avoid these conversations like the plague
Get drunk play pong
Nod your head
Get along

By all means join
The growing throng of lemmings
If your head is down
Perhaps
You'll never see the light dimming
But I can't breathe

There's a noose around my throat
That slightly loosens
If I smile and don't speak

I've got a choice to hang in peace
Or cut the rope
And watch eyes bulge
When on my feet

I think I'll choose the latter
I think I'll choose the latter
Rather than patter
And pander banter
Internalize micro-aggressions
And slander

While the blood splatters
In elegant patterns

You compliment me
On my oh so eloquent manner
Marvel that I grasp words
But won't address the candor
Damn sir

I'd rather not yes ma'am her

When you can hear the clamor
Shrieks and screams
Hoarse coarse choking screeches
Just beyond the outer reaches
Of the screen

I can't breathe

The gears of this machine
Run on fear & greed of the obscene
Somehow every bloody rag
Still comes out pristine
Whistling clean
Clean as a Whistle

Clean as a misguided missile
Or a bullet
From a pistol
Or the sizzle
Of burning flesh
That might make your stomach
Turn and retch

Unless you liked it

The burning wretch
You poked to death
Got you excited

Like a picnic
In your Sunday best
All invited
To view the grand parade of death
Still I can't breathe

Is this new
The coming attraction
Feature presentation
Or sneak preview

I just know my eyes are glued

There's a reason or excuse
To kill me
Anywhere I breathe
I tell you what
You can say nigger for a year

If you commit your life to end this vice
And convert all your racist peers

But maybe you like this beef too much
And can't steer
So you swerve
With the herd
To serve whatever dreams deferred this year

But I know you can do the math

Add each haunting tale of past to what is here
Making Black Lives Matter
More than just a hash tag and veneer
At least in your own sphere
Multiply the gasps by each last tear

Tell the people on the train the gas is near
Tell the people on the train the gas is near

Rajnii Eddins breathes through the written word. A full recital that allows us to see more clearly the dimly lit spaces of the black romantic. For over 2 decades, this poet, father, teacher and son has allowed the spoken word to be a guide and refuge. In his words, there is refuge for which I always felt drawn. When I'm with Rajnii, I often feel strong in his silence and watch him craft truth as he lives such that listening, breathing and writing become synonymous. It's rare that the light of hope shines so brightly these days and when it does we must stand forward and receive the light, lest we in our efforts, grow dim. Rajnii shares the long awaited letter from your dearest friend, your closest sister and the villain who attempts to steal our laughter. If you ride these poems, you will arrive at peace.

Thank you Raj for your light.

-    Theaster Gates

CPSIA information can be obtained
at www.ICGtesting.com
Printed in the USA
LVHW072117251119
638399LV00001B/2/P

* 9 7 8 1 0 9 5 9 9 9 8 0 8 3 *